DEVELOPING A STRATEGY FOR

A POLITICAL CAMPAIGN

Melissa Banigan

Rosen
YA™
New York

Published in 2020 by The Rosen Publishing Group, Inc.
29 East 21st Street, New York, NY 10010

First Edition

Library of Congress Cataloging-in-Publication Data

Name: Banigan, Melissa, author.
Title: Developing a strategy for a political campaign / Melissa Banigan.
Description: New York : Rosen Publishing, 2020 | Series: Be the change! Political
participation in your community | Includes bibliographical references and index. |
Audience: Grade 7 to 12.
Identifiers: LCCN 2019008479| ISBN 9781725340756 (library bound) |
ISBN 9781725340749 (pbk.)
Subjects: LCSH: Political campaigns—United States—Juvenile literature. | Campaign
management—United States—Juvenile literature. | Politics, Practical—United States—Juvenile
literature. | United States—Politics and government—20th century—Juvenile literature.
Classification: LCC JK2281 .B34 2019 | DDC 324.7/20973—dc23
LC record available at https://lccn.loc.gov/2019008479

Manufactured in the United States of America

CONTENTS

INTRODUCTION

After seventeen people were murdered during a shooting at Marjory Stoneman Douglas High School in Parkland, Florida, in 2018, Cameron Kasky, a student at the school, invited a few other students to his house to talk about how they could fight back against gun violence. They decided to start a movement called Never Again. Overnight, Never Again became an explosive political campaign that changed the conversation about gun violence in America, even prompting lawmakers in Florida to pass stricter gun control laws.

At first glance, it may seem like the Never Again campaign was destined to succeed. Kasky and his friends passionately denounced gun violence and millions of people across the country jumped on the bandwagon. Yet it takes a lot more than passion to convince lawmakers to write new policy or to elect politicians to office. Successful political campaigns also require a winning strategy—a plan of action designed to achieve a goal.

Consider the game of chess. Each player starts off with sixteen game pieces, including a king and a queen. The objective of the game is to capture the other player's king. Each player takes turns trying to attack and capture the other player's pieces on the board until one of the kings is finally taken. A winning

The Never Again movement became successful because the political strategy behind the movement combined a series of short-term actions and long-term goals with a powerful message.

strategy in chess is harder than it looks: players need to focus just as much on the goal of trying to capture the kings as they do on short-term actions. Together, the explicit goal of capturing the king and planning the moves that lead to that capture form the strategy of the game. The strategy of a political campaign is similar to a chess strategy in that one must consider both short- and long-term goals. The best campaign managers study and implement moves that have worked in other campaigns.

Cameron Kasky and the other teens who started Never Again wrote speeches that went viral, and their words inspired student walk-outs across the country and gained the support of celebrities. The teens even organized a demonstration in Washington, DC, called the March for Our Lives, and went on a national tour to encourage young people to register to vote. Yet it wasn't only the speeches, the walk-outs, or the celebrity attention that mattered, but rather the strategy that strung those things together. First, the teens developed a strong message—strengthening gun control laws to end mass murder in schools—that resonated with Americans from all walks of life. Second, the Never Again campaign was successful because it was open to anyone who wanted to join, so the number of people involved in the campaign kept growing, strengthening it further.

Laws don't get passed and presidents, council members, and even class presidents don't get elected without strategists who come up with a strong message and plan moves that can be implemented by a passionate group of campaigners. Learning how to develop a strategy for a political campaign can take you one step closer to spreading your message and winning the support of your community.

WHAT IS A POLITICAL CAMPAIGN?

olitical campaigns are designed to influence how a specific group of people makes decisions about issues or candidates who will be elected to office, and they are never simple. Most political campaigns are designed to appeal to a group of people's existing beliefs. For example, a Democratic campaign will generally appeal to people who identify as Democrats, while a Republican campaign will appeal to people who identify as Republicans.

Yet what happens when there are a number of people in the same political party who want to run for one office? Or when a candidate wants to push a bold new agenda? Or even when a group of teens wants to push the nation into passing new laws? In these cases, political strategists need to come up with ways to convince people that the ideas and messages of the campaign will benefit them.

It's not easy to convince someone to support a new idea, and it's especially hard to change a person's political beliefs. People's politics are strongly connected to their personal identities, and many people feel like they are being personally attacked when their political views are challenged. In fact, a 2016 study in the journal *Scientific Reports* suggests that people are resistant to arguments that contradict their political beliefs, even when those arguments are strongly backed by factual evidence. So a political campaign must also appeal to voters' emotions.

EVERYONE CAN PARTICIPATE IN A DEMOCRATIC CAMPAIGN

There are many kinds of political campaigns. In a democracy—a system of government in which all eligible members are allowed to vote for people to represent them—a campaign is often called an electoral campaign. "Electoral" refers to the word "electorate," which is all the people who are eligible to vote.

Electoral districts—the area in which a political campaign, election, and vote take place—can be villages, towns, cities, or countries. The people within these districts may identify as Democrats, Republicans, Greens, or Libertarians, or they may not be affiliated with any political party. Some members of the electorate may even decide not to vote, but that doesn't mean they're not a part of the electorate.

The biggest electoral campaigns focus on candidates who are running to become heads of state or heads of government, such as presidents and prime ministers. But there are all sorts of other electoral campaigns that support candidates running to sit on local school boards or city councils,

In 2018, Jack Bergeson and five other teenagers in Kansas participated in government by running for various political offices.

as well as county commissioners, justices of the peace, state representatives and senators, and governors.

If you think only adults are eligible to run for office, think again. Although the president of the United States is required to be at least thirty-five years old to sit in office, there isn't always an age limit for other offices. In 2018, a loophole allowed six teenagers to run for top offices in Kansas. Seventeen-year-old Jack Bergeson told ABC News that he decided to run as a Democratic candidate for governor because he didn't feel that either the Democratic or Republican Parties were addressing the right issues. While none of the

CAMPAIGN ADVICE FROM ANCIENT ROME

In 64 BCE, a lawyer and speaker named Cicero ran for the highest office in the Roman Republic and won. Yet he never would've succeeded without his brother, Quintus, who wrote a brilliant outline for a strategy that still holds two thousand years later. Below are just a few of the many kernels of wisdom that Quintus shared with his brother:

Flattery will get you everywhere: Quintus told his brother that he needed to learn the art of flattery, which means giving praise to serve one's own interests. He said, it's "a disgraceful thing in normal life but essential when you are running for office." Basically, this just means that candidates need to endear themselves to voters by making them feel important.

Give hope to the people: At the best and worst of times, Quintus thought it was important for voters to believe that his brother could help make Rome a better place. This policy makes sense in all political campaigns. After all, why would people want to vote for a candidate who makes them feel like the future is hopeless?

Flatter, give hope, and focus on an opponent's weakness—these were just a few pieces of advice Quintus gave his brother, Cicero, around two thousand years ago.

Attack an opponent's weaknesses: Quintus advised his brother to publicly attack his opponent's weakness—in this case, having problems with debt and also buying a slave. When people are focusing on a candidate's weaknesses, they won't focus so much on that person's strengths. The trick, however, is to avoid fighting dirty. While it's OK to talk about some of the things an opponent has done wrong, there are some big no-nos, such as smearing an opponent's family members.

young candidates won enough votes to sit in office, these teens inspired political conversations by running impressive, mature campaigns.

Even when young people aren't old enough to run for office or vote (the minimum legal voting age in the United States is eighteen), they can still develop or join political campaigns. In fact, young people of all ages are encouraged to participate in government, and there are even campaigns to lower the voting age to sixteen in local elections. This drive is based largely on research that shows that sixteen- and seventeen-year-olds are just as informed as older voters.

SUN TZU AND *THE ART OF WAR*

Sun Tzu grew up in ancient China during a period characterized by warfare and political unrest. A great military strategist, general, and philosopher, he wrote *The Art of War,* a text that shared a number of strategies for winning wars. He wrote, for example, that the biggest, strongest armies weren't always victorious. Forming strong alliances, using spies to collect information about enemies, and avoiding battles were just a few of the many strategies that could give smaller armies the competitive edge.

Sun Tzu didn't pull these strategies out of thin air. Instead, he analyzed the long history of war and discovered how battles had been won and lost. His careful study led him to discover that nearly everything he thought he knew about war was wrong. His strategies not only helped ancient China become more peaceful, but 2,500 years later, they've been used by countless great military strategists and politicians alike in Japan, the United States, and beyond.

Sun Tzu's story shows that political strategies not only help win battles, they can also change the world. Just as Sun Tzu studied history to glean wisdom, modern political campaigns also incorporate strategies that have a proven track record.

ABRAHAM LINCOLN: AN HONEST STRATEGY

In 2018, results taken from C-SPAN's third Presidential Historians Survey showed that Abraham Lincoln was voted the best president in American history. It might be surprising to learn that this respected Republican president almost wasn't reelected for a second term to office in 1864. Except for Andrew Jackson, no other president had won a second term in over three decades. The nation was in the midst of the Civil War and Americans were tired of all the bloodshed. Despite these strikes against him, Lincoln was committed to ending the war, abolishing slavery, and bringing unity to a divided country. So even though he didn't think he could win another election, he jumped into the race.

To gain support, Lincoln advised voters and potential political allies not to "change horses in the middle of a stream." Basically, he was asking people to give him more time to finish the work he had set out to do for the nation. Then, rather than hit the campaign trail to try to convince people to vote for him, he declined most invitations to speak, saying that people already knew his beliefs and what was at stake for the country.

This strategy may not have worked had it not been for Lincoln's reputation for honesty. He was committed to following the laws and believed in upholding the Constitution. His devotion to

Abraham Lincoln's reputation for being an honest and law-abiding man of his word helped him win a second term as president of the United States.

the law made people believe that he was honest and capable of sticking with the various promises he had made for the country. In the end, he won the election by a landslide.

Lincoln understood the importance of honesty as a campaign strategy. According to the *Journal of the Abraham Lincoln Association*, Lincoln told a Pennsylvania congressman, "All through the campaign my friends have been calling me 'honest Old Abe,' and I have been elected mainly on that cry."

BARACK OBAMA: GOING AFTER THE YOUTH VOTE

Politicians and the media alike spend a lot of time talking about the "youth vote," a term that describes young voters and their voting habits. In the United States, voter turnout for young people is lower than for most other groups within the electorate. In fact, according to the United States Census Bureau, only 46.1 percent of people ages eighteen to twenty-nine voted in the 2016 presidential election, compared to 70.9 percent of people over sixty-five, 66.6 percent of people between forty-five and sixty-four, and 58.7 percent of people between thirty and forty-four.

This problem can be attributed to a number of factors. Young people may have impediments to voting that their parents and grandparents often don't have. Some don't have transportation to get to their polling site, or the process of registering may feel too difficult or confusing due to complicated voter registration laws. Other young people wonder why they should bother, as they feel like politicians don't really focus on their concerns.

In 2008, however, over 50 percent of young people voted in the presidential election, according to CIRCLE (the Center for Information and Research on Civic Learning and Engagement). Of these young voters, 66 percent voted for the Democratic candidate, Barack Obama.

Barack Obama's campaign strategy during both of his presidential campaigns involved listening to young people and going after the youth vote.

Many candidates only pander to young people. Obama, however, really listened to their concerns and insisted that they become important stakeholders in his campaign. This strategy not only helped him win the election in 2008, it also got him reelected in 2012.

CHAPTER TWO

HOW TO GET PEOPLE TO LISTEN

There's no point in creating a strategy for a political campaign without having a message people want to hear. What does a candidate have to say that will resonate with large numbers of people? Which issues will a campaign focus on? These are important questions that must be answered before a political campaign even begins.

FOCUSING ON THE THINGS THAT MATTER

Twenty-eight-year-old Democratic Socialist Alexandria Ocasio-Cortez was an unknown political outsider when she beat longtime US representative Joe Crowley in the primary for his seat in New York's Fourteenth Congressional District, covering parts of the Bronx and Queens, in 2018. A year before her win, she worked as a bartender, leaving many people to wonder, how on earth did she do it?

For starters, Ocasio-Cortez chose issues that mattered to her base of voters. One of her key

Political outsider Alexandria Ocasio-Cortez focused on issues that resonated with voters, including finding better ways to handle immigration policies.

campaign issues was to "abolish ICE." Abolish ICE is a political movement that seeks to shut down Immigration and Customs Enforcement (ICE), a government agency within the Department of Homeland Security that is responsible for detaining and deporting undocumented immigrants. Ocasio-Cortez believed that ICE punished and hurt immigrants, and she called on government leaders to find a more humane way to enforce immigration policies.

Many people living in the district were recent immigrants from countries such as Mexico and

Bangladesh, among others. Abolishing ICE was a particularly important issue for these people, who feared being targeted by the agency. Dozens of volunteers in Ocasio-Cortez's campaign went door to door, visiting more than ten thousand homes in Queens to discuss their candidate's desire to abolish ICE. Many people related to this message, and it helped Ocasio-Cortez receive a tremendous amount of local and national attention—enough attention to win Crowley's seat in Congress.

THREE STEPS TO CREATING A STRONG MESSAGE

All campaigns must have a strong message that resonates with voters, but how are these strong messages developed? The following are three steps used by political campaigners:

Short and sweet: If a message is too long, it won't be memorable. Yet it should still pack a powerful punch. Think of the most important message you want to convey to voters, then work on finding the simplest way to say it.

Telling the truth: Telling the truth is always a good strategy, and in a campaign message, it holds particular importance. The political messages that go down in history as changing the world for the better—like the ones that charged the civil rights movement, for example—are always backed by truth.

Repeating the message: Most people have had the experience of getting song lyrics stuck in their head after hearing a song dozens of times. The same thing happens with a strong political message: hear it once and people might not remember it. Hear it multiple times and it will start to sink in. It might even convince people to vote for a candidate. That's why it's vital for a political campaign to repeat its message ... over and over again.

UNDERSTANDING VOTERS

Just as advertising campaigns can convince people that one brand of soap is better than the others, promoting a candidate's political message, ideals, and issues is a vital part of winning an election. However, it's not enough just to create advertisements about a candidate. Political strategists first need to understand the needs, desires, and hardships of potential voters, then they can target those voters through advertising. Product marketers of baby food, for example, don't share their ads on websites targeted to children, because it's parents, not kids, who buy the product! In the same way, political campaigns don't place advertisements about issues important to young

To win an election, political strategists must first get to know the things that matter most to different groups of potential voters.

parents in magazines for retired people—it just doesn't make sense.

Learning what makes voters tick is one of the most important parts of any political campaign, no matter whether it's a student election or a presidential election. To learn how to communicate with voters, great political strategists spend countless hours poring over a few key pieces of data about voters: voter segments, demographics, and party affiliations.

VOTER SEGMENTS

Think about an orange. It has many pieces, or segments, that form the entire piece of fruit. The same philosophy is true for voter segments in that there are many groups of distinct voters who form the whole electorate. Registered voters, for example, are a voter segment of people who have registered to vote, while likely voters are people who are actually predicted to vote in an election.

There are many voter segments. Each year, new ones are created. For example, women became a new voter segment when they were finally given the right to vote in 1920. Millennials—the demographic of people born between approximately 1980 and 1990—became a voter segment when they turned eighteen years old.

It's important for political campaign managers to understand every one of the voter segments. If a campaign tries to share a message that doesn't impact all voter segments, they might lose votes. Learning more about the concerns of separate voter segments can be done through polling. This practice means asking questions of many people within a voter segment to discover their opinions about various issues.

DEMOGRAPHICS

Demographics are the characteristics of groups of people. Some characteristics include age, race, gender, marital status, number of children, education level, and income level. Demographic information is often collected through statistics, which is a type of math focused on collecting, organizing, and interpreting data.

Different voter segments often have different demographics. For example, the demographic of older voters who have retired from their jobs will probably have different needs than the demographic of voters who have just turned eighteen years old. People with young children will have different needs than those who don't have children.

Different demographics often have different voting habits. This difference can impact the voter segments a political campaign chooses to target. For example, voter turnout among young voters is often much lower than that of older voters. In the United States, there are also more white people voting in elections than black people. This factor means that many politicians focus predominantly on the issues of older, white demographics. This priority isn't fair, as it often means that political campaigns—and government in general—cater to the needs of some demographics more than others.

There are two major political parties, as well as many smaller ones, each with its own goals. Different demographics of voters often vote along different party lines.

PARTY AFFILIATION

The Democratic Party, Republican Party, Green Party of the United States, and Libertarian Party are just a few of the political parties in the United States, although the two major parties in government are the Democratic Party and the Republican Party. Each of these parties has its own political goals, and they organize to help candidates get elected to various public offices, from city council to the presidency.

Many voters vote along party lines, which means they choose candidates from one party over the others, which is called being affiliated with a party. Different demographics and segments of voters often have different party affiliations. For example, in 2019 the Democratic Party had more voters who were people of color, millennials, and had college degrees, while the Republican Party had more voters who were white men without college degrees.

DEVELOPING A DREAM TEAM

During a theatrical play, an audience generally only sees the actors on the stage. Yet people like the director, playwright, and even volunteer ushers are fundamental to the success of any performance. The same goes for a political campaign: a candidate cannot win an election alone—a political campaign is only as strong as its campaign staff, political consultants, volunteers, and activists who stand behind it.

CAMPAIGN STAFF

Depending on the campaign, there may be between many hundreds and many thousands of staff on a presidential campaign's payroll. In 2016, for example, the campaign for the Democratic nominee, Hillary Clinton, had 4,800 people on staff, while the Republican nominee, Donald Trump's, campaign had eight hundred. Most political campaigns won't require nearly as many people, but even the smallest campaigns benefit from having the following staff members:

Campaign manager: The person chosen to fill this role manages staff and volunteers and coordinates all campaign operations, including fundraising, volunteering, advertising, and event planning.

Campaign fundraiser: All campaigns require money. Campaign fundraisers create fundraising plans for campaigns, and they help figure out how much money goes toward various initiatives within the campaign.

Volunteer coordinator: Imagine showing up as a volunteer at a local shelter for homeless people and having no one there to tell you what to do or how to help. Having a designated person to manage and coordinate volunteers helps every volunteer know where to go, what to do, and how to help.

POLITICAL CONSULTANTS

Consultants are people who lend their expertise to individuals or organizations. A political consultant is a person who advises candidates and political campaign staffers on many aspects of a campaign. Jobs may include organizing various media communications efforts, and they most often include helping to make voters aware of the campaign message and the reasons why they should vote for the candidate.

Steve Schmidt is an example of a successful political consultant. Specializing in strategy and the development of strong campaign messages, he worked on big Republican political campaigns for George W. Bush, Arnold Schwarzenegger, and John McCain. As journalist Holly Bailey wrote in an article for *Newsweek*,

Even when they're too young to vote, teenagers can volunteer on political campaigns to help the candidates of their choice get elected to office.

"Schmidt's signature practice is to pick a simple message and repeat it day after day until it begins to sink in with the public."

Joseph Napolitan is credited with being the first person to call himself a political consultant. He worked on more than one hundred American political campaigns, including the 1960 presidential campaign of John F. Kennedy and the 1968 campaign of Hubert Humphrey. In 1969, he founded the American Association of Political Consultants, which is the world's largest organization of political consultants. The organization offers awards every year to people under the age of forty who are in the political business community. It's a great resource for people wanting to learn more about consultants.

VOLUNTEERS AND ACTIVISTS

According to an April 2018 article in the *Washington Post*, one in five Americans had participated in political rallies or protested since the beginning of 2016. Many of these activists are young people. They are the foot soldiers who canvass door to door, make phone calls, help plan and run events, and take part in a slew of other important activities that help candidates get elected.

In 1978, Claudine Schneider understood the importance of having volunteers and activists join her campaign to become the first woman to win a Republican seat in Congress in the state of Rhode Island. During the campaign, reporters said to Schneider, "Look, you're young, you're a woman, you have no money, you have no name-recognition. How do you possibly expect to win?" Her answer? Grow the number of volunteers working on her campaign.

A friend of Schneider's husband came up with a club called the Claudine 15s. When supporters contributed $15 to the campaign, volunteered fifteen hours, and talked to fifteen other people about Schneider, they received a campaign button that showed that they were a part of the club. Schneider lost the election, but she had formed such a strong coalition of volunteers that, when she ran again two years later, she won, becoming the first congresswoman to represent Rhode Island.

CHAPTER THREE

WINNING A POLITICAL POPULARITY CONTEST

Political campaigns are often like popularity contests: the candidate who is the most liked by the electorate wins. In 2000, Republican George W. Bush and Democrat Vice President Al Gore ran against each other in a race for the office of president of the United States. According to a poll conducted by CNN, *USA Today*, and Gallup, Bush and Gore seemed evenly matched based on a number of big governmental issues.

Yet the poll also showed that voters believed that Bush had a stronger character than his opponent. In fact, he was not only considered more "honest and

Although George W. Bush narrowly won enough electoral votes to become president in 2000, Al Gore won the popular vote. Gore might've won more votes had he been deemed more "likable."

trustworthy," but also more "likable" than Gore. After a very contentious race, Bush narrowly won enough of the electoral votes needed to win the election.

Although the results of the 2000 election were dependent on a lot more than the likability of one candidate over the other, it's possible that the history books might show a different story if Gore had been liked by more voters. In politics, popularity matters, and campaigns need to focus on making candidates as attractive as possible to voters.

THE SCIENCE OF STUDYING POLITICS, SOCIETY, AND PEOPLE

Political science is the study of politics, sociology is the study of society, and psychology is the study of the way the human mind works. In a political campaign, smart campaign managers and consultants often turn to researchers and scientists to help them learn more about the issues that are important to voters as well as how best to talk about those issues.

It's important to make impactful campaign ads. Many people used to assume that positive, upbeat ads had the greatest impact on voters, but according to an article by Sadie Dingfelder in APA's *Monitor on Psychology* magazine, a 2005 study actually showed that negative ads performed the best. Images of smiling children and waving American flags simply didn't hold viewer interest nearly as much as depictions of violence. The study showed that fear made people reconsider whom to vote for, while happy, positive

A little science can go a long way toward helping win a political election. Surveys, polls, and focus groups are scientific methods that can even be used in school elections.

ads simply made them feel more comfortable with the choice they had already made.

The study goes to show that making assumptions about people can hurt a campaign, while scientific study can help campaigns come up with new winning strategies. The good news is that campaigns don't need to turn to political scientists for help. The following scientific methods can be used by anyone!

SURVEYS AND POLLS

Conducted by asking multiple-choice questions, a political poll helps campaigners find out important information about voters. Responses to the question, "Whom will you vote for in the election?" for example, may show campaign staff how likely it would be for their candidate to win or lose the election on that particular day.

Yet efficient polling is more complicated than that. It is possible to find out the answer to the question "Whom will you vote for in the election?" by asking many other questions about the candidates and their issues. In addition to showing which candidate is preferred, poll results may offer illuminating information about the ways in which each candidate is valued. People who develop and run polls—pollsters—are highly valued when they demonstrate a history of creating effective polls.

FOCUS GROUPS

Focus groups let campaign staff test their messages with small groups of real people. Let's say a candidate for class president wants to test the idea of serving more salad in school lunches. Rather than ask every single person in the school for their views on school lunch and salad, the candidate might instead speak to a handful of people—a couple from each homeroom— to get a sense of how the school feels as a whole.

Focus groups are important because they let campaign staffers test many messages at once. As one focus group, for example, discusses the benefits of more salads being offered in school lunches, other focus groups might be picking apart other topics, such as serving less salad in school lunches, serving only organic food in school lunches, or starting a garden at the school. The information collected by these focus groups can provide valuable information to candidates about how to strengthen their overall message about school lunches.

DISCRIMINATION MAKES SOME CANDIDATES MORE POPULAR THAN OTHERS

In 2016, Democrat Hillary Clinton narrowly lost the presidential election against her opponent, Republican Donald Trump. In the months after the election, many politicians, academics, journalists, and other thinkers wondered if Clinton had lost at least in part because she was a woman. In a paper titled "The Impact of 'Modern Sexism' on the 2016 Presidential Election," based on polling done by the Diane D. Blair Center of Southern Politics & Society at the University of Arkansas, researchers reported the results of a poll showing that many voters didn't vote for Clinton based on her gender.

Women aren't the only group discriminated against by voters. A 2017 study from the Stanford University Graduate School of Business showed that delegates who were people of color received an estimated 10 percent fewer votes than white delegates bound

Although many people feel discrimination was a factor in keeping a woman out of the Oval Office in 2016, more voters than ever before are choosing candidates who aren't white men.

to the same candidate during Republican presidential primaries in Illinois.

Fortunately, many candidates and voters are fighting back against discrimination. For example, in 2018, more transgender people than ever before ran for office. Two of these candidates, Lisa Bunker and Gerri Cannon, both Democrats, won campaigns to serve in New Hampshire's House of Representatives. And although Clinton didn't win her bid for president, a record number of women (102) were elected to serve in the 116th Congress in 2018, and there were more people of color serving in the House of Representatives than ever before.

★ SOCIAL MEDIA FOR THE WIN—HOW THE
★ INTERNET CHANGED POLITICAL CAMPAIGNS

Politicians used to rely only on traditional media (newspapers, radio, and TV) to cover their campaigns, but the internet has changed the way people do just about everything, including how candidates spread their messages. The following are a number of strategies for using social media in a political campaign.

Develop a goal: First, figure out the purpose of your social media campaign. Is the goal to make a candidate appear more likable to a particular demographic of voters? Is it to tell voters how candidates would work on a particular issue if they were elected to office? Developing an end goal helps social media strategists target the right audience.

Create a content calendar: Writing a few social media posts isn't enough. Social media should tell stories that will help the campaign meet its goal. Writing out a calendar containing a week, a month, or even a few months of content helps campaign managers stay organized and make sure their posts develop a story over time.

Create great content: Different social media channels require different kinds of content. For example, Facebook is great for sharing posts with links to articles, while Instagram is useful for creating and sharing short video stories. Great social media content is typically short and sweet, and often includes images, video clips, and memes. All content should support the original goal of the social media campaign.

Schedule posts: After creating a goal, a content calendar, and terrific content, it's time to share posts. Weekdays are generally the best days to post, with Tuesday through Thursday generating the most views.

All of this goes to show that, although discrimination still makes minority candidates a less popular choice than white men, more and more voters are starting to choose candidates based on their merits rather than factors such as gender and race.

MAKING A CANDIDATE MORE LIKABLE

During a political campaign, everything about a candidate's message, issues, and personality are scrutinized. There's no exact science to making a person seem more appealing to an entire electorate, but a strong formula typically includes fundraising, science, and attracting the attention of as many potential voters as possible. The most popular attention-grabbing endeavors include the following:

Grassroots organizing is a great way to get out into the community to meet voters face to face. Activities can include calling voters, passing out campaign materials, and simply talking to members of the community.

Community support: Asking volunteers to get out in the neighborhood is a great way to meet voters face to face. Also called field organizing or grassroots organizing, community activities may include calling registered voters on the phone, handing out leaflets, or organizing events.

Going door to door: In smaller campaigns, volunteers and even candidates may also stop at the homes of registered voters to share their message. On Election Day, these door-to-door visits—also called canvassing—will help voters remember the candidates as well as increase the chance that they'll remember specific issues that may influence their vote.

Receiving endorsements from influencers and celebrities: Research published in the *Journal of Political Marketing* in 2018 showed that celebrity endorsements of political candidates can matter a lot. For example, in the run-up to the 2018 midterm elections, singer Taylor Swift endorsed two Democratic candidates in her home state of Tennessee. Journalist Rosa Inocencio Smith wrote in *The Atlantic* that within twenty-four hours of Swift's endorsement, a website called Vote.org reported sixty-five thousand new registered voters.

When celebrities share their endorsements of candidates, their fans are more likely to vote for that person. This situation doesn't mean, however, that all campaigns need megacelebrities to back their candidates. Political campaigns in schools may want to ask the head of the debate club, star football quarterback, or other popular students for their support.

MONEY, MONEY, MONEY

Not many political campaigns will succeed without cold, hard cash. While presidential campaigns require millions of dollars even to get off the ground, student campaigns might need only a little money for making some campaign posters. There are many laws that regulate how campaigns manage donations, money, and spending. All campaign and fundraising managers—whether they're part of a small school or large national campaign—should take some time orienting themselves to the laws as they create their campaign finance plans.

HOW TO COVER CAMPAIGN EXPENSES

A big consideration for any political campaign is whether it will have enough money to operate. Campaigns can be expensive, but with some careful planning and a strong fundraising strategy, a campaign improves its chances of winning an election.

CREATING AN OPERATING BUDGET

Whether a campaign has millions of dollars or zero cents, creating a realistic plan for a budget is the first step to figuring out how to cover campaign expenses. In fact, campaign managers should consider the budget long before kicking off the campaign or fundraising so much as a dime. Without a budget, campaign organizers won't know how much money to allocate to things like advertising or salaries.

The goal of a political campaign is to win votes for the candidate. Therefore, every dollar budgeted in the campaign should help achieve this goal. Campaign managers and fundraisers need to consider all of the

Political campaigns require a budget so that they not only know how much money they have, but how many dollars they can devote to various campaign expenses.

campaign operations and then figure out how much each of those things costs. Does a campaign plan on sending volunteers door to door to collect signatures and email addresses from registered voters? If so, the cost of pens, clipboards, and the printing of forms should be included in the budget. Nothing— not even a box of pens—should be left out. Once the budget is approved and money is being spent, it's the responsibility of the campaign organizers to record what every cent is spent on.

FUNDRAISING

Is the idea of asking people to contribute to a political campaign intimidating? Well, get over it. Many people consider making contributions to a campaign a way of helping their favored candidates become the public servants who will represent their interests. Therefore, a dollar, a few dollars, or sometimes even thousands of dollars often feels worth it to them.

The first step to fundraising is setting a fundraising goal. How much money does the campaign already have? How much does the budget need? Subtract one from the other to figure out how much you need to raise.

Fundraising can take many forms, from mailing letters of appeal to hosting events to using online fundraising platforms. This is the time to get creative. Think of the people who support the campaign. Is there a famous singer or popular restaurant owner who hopes the candidate will win? Ask these people to host concerts, dinners, or other fundraising events.

Fundraising can feel intimidating, but even a few dollars can help a political campaign. Many candidates host fundraising events to solicit donations from enthusiastic supporters.

What about a local carwash or other business? Perhaps they'd consider hosting a day where they donate a dime for every dollar they earn to the campaign.

Once the money starts rolling in, just remember to record who made donations, and how much they gave, then thank every single one of those people. In the future, these same people may want to contribute again to help the candidates they like win an election.

REGULATIONS ABOUT POLITICAL FINANCE

Although money is often vital for democratic politics, there must be regulations to ensure that corruption (dishonest behavior) and fraud (criminal deception) are prevented. One of the biggest cases of campaign

★ WHAT IS A SUPER PAC?

In the United States and Canada, political action committees, or PACs, were created to raise money privately from individuals. These funds (which used to be between $1,000 and $2,500) were donated to a political campaign to support or defeat a political candidate.

Before 2010, corporations and unions weren't allowed to raise money or donate funds to influence federal elections. This practice meant that PACs could accept only limited contributions from individuals, and they weren't allowed to take money from groups.

This situation changed in 2010 when a couple of court cases found the ban against unlimited funds unconstitutional. The first of these cases (*Citizens United v. Federal Election Commission*) is often referred to as Citizens United, while the other court ruling is called *Speechnow.org v. Federal Election Commission*.

In 2019, there were nearly 1,300 registered super PACs, each with its own agenda. These PACs can do many of the things actual campaigns do, including calling registered voters and running ad campaigns. Super PACs can greatly impact campaigns, and many people believe they give an unfair advantage to the wealthy donors who are able to contribute millions of dollars.

finance corruption in America is the Watergate scandal. In 1972, five men were arrested for breaking into the Democratic National Committee headquarters in the Watergate building in Washington, DC. Soon after the arrest, a Federal Bureau of Investigation (FBI) investigation discovered a link between the thieves and money used by a committee to help reelect Republican president Richard Nixon. The mismanagement of campaign funds led to the president resigning from office, and it also forced the country to reexamine its campaign finance laws.

Following campaign finance laws not only is the right thing to do, it also keeps people out of jail. For example, in 2018, President Donald Trump's former lawyer Michael Cohen was sentenced to three years in prison for paying out an illegal campaign donation during the president's campaign.

Campaign finance corruption is a big deal. Republican president Richard Nixon had to resign from office due to the gross mismanagement of campaign funds by his reelection committee.

In the United States, campaign finance law is different at federal, state, and local levels. Federal finance law is written and enacted by Congress and is enforced by a government agency called the Federal Election Commission, while nonfederal campaigns are enacted and enforced by state and local lawmakers. There are many state-by-state variations of the law. Ballotpedia is a great nonpartisan political resource for learning more information about various campaign finance requirements.

CHAPTER FIVE

PULLING IT ALL TOGETHER

Does your campaign have a great message that goes over well in focus groups? Check. What about issues that matter to the majority of the electorate? Check. Does it have a realistic budget and fundraising plan? Check. Now that all of these things are in place, the campaign is really just getting started.

WORKING TOWARD CAMPAIGN GOALS

Although the primary objective of a campaign is to win the race, shorter-term goals also need to be set after the campaign launches. This step is necessary largely because, before a campaign, it's often difficult to know exactly who else will run in the election.

In 2016, there were seventeen Republican candidates vying for the office of president of the United States, each with their own interests. There probably aren't as many candidates running for the same office in school elections across the country, but it's still important to know all the candidates and learn about the issues they stand behind. How many prospective voters also think those issues are important? More important, do voters think the issues supported by the other campaign are important? What about the message, various slogans, and the likability of candidates? Which candidates appear to capture the imagination of voters?

Campaigns are fluid, meaning they are always moving and always changing. This situation means that campaigns should continue to conduct polls throughout the campaign, rather than relying on information gathered from one poll. Public opinion can change quickly, and a campaign should try to stay one step ahead of it.

The biggest rule of thumb for running a successful campaign is to have candidates listen more than they talk. After all, the campaign really has very little to do

Political candidates don't win elections unless they listen to voters. This is why candidates should talk only when necessary and always be careful to stay on message.

with the candidates—it has everything to do with the voters. If the electorate doesn't think that a candidate is listening to their concerns, they won't vote for that candidate. Therefore, candidates should talk only when necessary and only when they're sharing their messages and discussing the issues that voters want to hear about. This strategy is called staying on message.

FOCUSING ON THE END GAME

It's impossible for campaign organizers to do everything they want to do. Even with a large staff and many months to campaign, there are always too few people and too little time. Being strategic about how to use volunteers and campaign finances becomes even more important close to Election Day, when it's especially vital to be reaching voters. Many of the decisions a campaign manager makes in the final days of the campaign will aim to maximize the resources and time that are left. For example, if there's only a week left in the campaign, it may be tough to reach out to every single voter. Figuring out whom to target is key.

TARGETING PEOPLE WHO ACTUALLY VOTE

In 2017, the Stanford University Graduate School of Business published a report showing that public outreach by political campaigns doesn't win votes from undecided voters and people who support other candidates. This finding means that advertising and door-to-door canvassing have very little impact unless a voter already supports a campaign's candidate.

This information doesn't mean, however, that campaigns shouldn't actively send volunteers door to door or try to convince voters about the merits of a particular candidate. Instead, it means that campaigns need to be selective in the voters they target.

Not all registered voters vote. Since 1950, the polling company Gallup has been identifying which registered voters are most likely to vote during presidential elections. Targeting this voter segment rather than all eligible voters is one way to maximize a campaign's time and resources.

WINNING OVER PEOPLE WHO DON'T VOTE

Although some campaigns spend more time targeting only likely voters, other campaigns and political activists also try to win over people who typically don't vote. For example, although there are more eligible voters under the age of thirty than there are over sixty-five, younger people are less likely to vote than older people. In 2018, a group of fifteen Generation Z youth (a generation of people born between the mid-1990s and the early 2000s) created an online political campaign using videos to urge people in their generation to vote.

This campaign, called #WhyDoYouVote, was the brainchild of Hollywood filmmaker Darren Aronofsky and a nonprofit called the Sierra Club, and it was organized by young people such as climate change activist Xiuhtezcatl Martinez, immigrant rights activist Lisbeth Chavarria, and Parkland shooting survivor David Hogg.

Celebrities also organized events to urge young people to vote—singer Taylor Swift, for example, asked

Young people are less likely to vote than older people. The #WhyDoYouVote campaign was organized to urge some of these young people to head to the polls.

her 112 million followers on Instagram to vote. The combined efforts of campaigns such as #WhyDoYouVote and celebrity endorsements were wildly successful. As Julie Beck reported in *The Atlantic*, the youth vote surged by 188 percent during the 2018 midterm elections, compared to 2014, showing that while it might seem safer to go after only likely voters, going after voter segments and demographics of people who don't usually vote can also have a big impact.

CAPTURING THE IMAGINATION OF VOTERS

It's not enough to appeal to voters simply based on the issues they care about. It's also vital to appeal to their hearts. Barack Obama's 2008 presidential campaign, for example, appealed to voters' hearts by using the words, "Yes we can." These three words reminded people of how Obama was defying the odds by running to become the first black president of the United States. They captured the imagination of voters from all walks of life who also believed they could beat the odds, and they even appeared in a music video by will.i.am.

Obama wasn't the first person to appeal to voters' hearts. Democratic president John F. Kennedy's We Can Do Better slogan also struck a chord with the electorate, as did Republican president Ronald Reagan's slogan, Let's Make America Great Again. This last slogan was later revived by Donald Trump's campaign during his successful bid for the presidency in 2016.

In 2018, women running for local and national government offices challenged voters to consider a world where men and women were treated fairly. Republican Martha McSally (Arizona) launched her campaign for the Senate by instructing Republicans in Washington to "grow a pair of ovaries." Meanwhile, Democratic gubernatorial candidates Kelda Roys (Wisconsin) and Krish Vignarajah (Maryland) breastfed their babies in campaign advertisements to show that mothers could also be leaders.

Strong political candidates have great ideas—it's the job of a political campaign to take those ideas, break them down into a handful of words and images, and use them to capture the imagination of voters.

HOW TO AVOID FAKE NEWS TO WIN ELECTIONS

It's not enough to develop communications and social media strategies. Earned media (the press) also has a big role to play in a political campaign, as it ultimately helps to tell a campaign's story. Therefore, it is vital to form relationships with the press—but only with media outlets that are honest and adhere to high journalistic standards.

It is common to hear politicians, journalists, teachers, and many other people talk about "fake news." But what is this phenomenon and how can it be avoided? Fake news is simply news that contains information that isn't true. It's often written with the purpose of deliberately misleading people, but sometimes it's published when journalists, news outlets, or social media users aren't thoroughly fact-checking to make sure all of the information they're sharing is true.

Fortunately, there are many news outlets that have very high journalistic standards—in other words, they work hard to tell the truth. Before campaign staffers speak with any members of the press, they should learn how to spot fake news by considering the following issues:

Consider the source: Before believing everything in an article, step back for a minute and think about the source. Is it a well-known media publication? Does it have a reputation for being honest?

Check the author or journalist: Who wrote the article? Do a quick search on Google to see if the journalist's name pops up. Is this person credible? Has he or she published other work? Many fake news journalists have fake names and won't have a big online presence.

Check the date: If it's a current news story, then the date should also be current.

Make sure in-story sources add up: OK, so the source seems real and the author's name checks

Fake news is news that is released to mislead people. It can have serious negative consequences during elections, but, fortunately, there are some ways it can be spotted.

out. To dig a little deeper, click on each link found in a story. Where do the links lead? Hopefully to other reputable sources!

Learn the difference between news and satire: Fake news misleads, while satire uses humor to expose or ridicule truths about people, organizations, candidates, and even governments. The book *Animal Farm*, by George Orwell, for example, used characters who were farm animals to expose truths about a form of government called totalitarianism (which, as the name suggests, imposes total control over individuals).

Look it up on a fact-checking site: Not sure how to find out if a source is honest? Then look it up on a fact-checking website. Many of these sites are acclaimed for being unbiased. Try PolitiFact, Snopes, Factcheck .org, Open Secrets, and the *Washington Post*'s Fact Checker.

WHAT HAPPENS AFTER ELECTION DAY?

It's always worth getting involved in a political campaign. It's a great way to learn about political systems, elections, and the issues that are important to various demographics and voter segments. None of these lessons end on Election Day.

No matter whether a candidate wins or loses an election, it's important to end on a positive note. Every single person who worked on the campaign should be thanked, from volunteers to campaign managers. People who contributed money to the campaign should also be thanked. This courtesy isn't only gracious, it's good strategy. Keeping supporters in the good graces of a campaign means they can be called upon in the future to help with other campaigns.

Although campaigns are supposed to spend all of the money fundraised during the campaign, sometimes there is still some unspent cash. In a school campaign, it's important to ask the school leadership for their advice. Sometimes the answer of what to do with leftover money is as simple as donating it to a good cause or buying pizza for the student body.

In bigger campaigns, especially at the federal level, what to do with leftover campaign money is a little more

Election Day is an exciting time. After a campaign ends, thoughtful candidates always thank the people who worked to help get them elected.

complicated. The Federal Election Commission has very strict rules on what can and cannot be done with the funds. For example, candidates can't simply take the money for their own use. They can, however, donate the funds to charity or even give a certain amount to other candidates. The money can also be saved in a special account to use if the candidate plans to run for office again.

Whether a candidate wins or loses, it's important to remember that the next election is right around the corner!

bias Prejudice in favor of one thing, group, or person.

democracy A system of government in which all eligible people vote for elected officials to represent them in government.

Democrat A member of the Democratic Party, one of the two major political parties in the United States.

demographics Characteristics of groups of people, such as age, race, gender, or income.

electoral Relating to the electorate or elections.

electorate All the people in a specific area or country who are eligible to vote.

pander To indulge a person's needs or desires.

political campaign The means by which political candidates try to appeal to voters in the run-up to an election.

political message A carefully constructed statement that candidates, political campaign staff, and other stakeholders share with voters.

political strategy A plan of action designed to achieve a political goal, such as to elect a candidate to office.

politician A person who is professionally involved in politics, often as an elected official.

Republican A member of the Republican Party, one of the two major political parties in the United States.

volunteer A person who performs a service without compensation.

voter segment A distinct group of voters that is part of an electorate.

youth vote Young voters and their voting habits.

American Association of Political Consultants
8400 Westpark Drive
McLean, VA 22102
(703) 245-8020
Website: https://theaapc.org
Facebook: @AAPCFans
Twitter: @TheAAPC
A multipartisan organization, the American Association
of Political Consultants has a global membership
of political and media consultants, congressional
staffers, and many other political professionals who
work to uphold democracy.

Ballotpedia
8383 Greenway Boulevard, Suite 600
Middleton, WI 53562
(608) 255-0688
Website: https://ballotpedia.org
Facebook: @Ballotpedia
Twitter: @ballotpedia
Ballotpedia is a nonpartisan digital encyclopedia and
nonprofit organization that includes entries about
American political policy from federal to local levels.

British Columbia Youth Parliament (BCYP)
509 - 1383 Marinaside Crescent
Vancouver, BC V62 2W9
Canada
(604) 646-6623
Website: http://www.bcyp.org
Facebook: @bcyouthparliament
Instagram and Twitter: @bcyparliament

British Columbia Youth Parliament is a youth service organization modeled on the Westminster Parliamentary system.

CIRCLE (The Center for Information & Research on Civic Learning and Engagement)
Jonathan M. Tisch College of Civic Life
10 Upper Campus Road
Lincoln Filene Hall
Tufts University
Medford, MA 02155
(617) 627-3453
Website: http://civicyouth.org
Facebook: @Center-for-Information-Research-on-Civic-Learning-and-Engagement-CIRCLE
Twitter: @CivicYouth
CIRCLE (The Center for Information & Research on Civic Learning and Engagement) helps increase civil engagement of young people and works to change policy that affects marginalized youth.

PolitiFact (at the Poynter Institute)
1100 Connecticut Avenue NW, Suite 1300B
Washington, DC 20036
Website: https://www.politifact.com
Facebook and Twitter: @politifact
Managed by the Poynter Institute (a nonprofit journalism and media research center), PolitiFact is a fact-checking website that gives statements in the media a Truth-O-Meter rating. Ratings range from True (for statements that are accurate) to Pants on Fire (for statements that are inaccurate or ridiculous).

Rock the Vote
1440 G Street NW
Washington, DC 20005
(202) 719-9910
Website: https://www.rockthevote.org
Facebook, Instagram, and Twitter: @rockthevote
Rock the Vote is a nonpartisan and progressive
nonprofit organization that uses music, pop culture,
and art to motivate young people to get involved in
politics, build their political power, and make voting
work for everyone.

Student Vote
Canada
Website: http://studentvote.ca
Facebook and Twitter: @studentvote
Instagram: @civix_canada
Student Vote runs mock elections for students under
the voting age. It also provides electoral education
in schools and materials for families.

Youth Service America (YSA)
1050 Connecticut Avenue NW, Room 65525
Washington, DC 20036
(202) 296-2992
Website: https://ysa.org/vote
Facebook: @youthserviceamerica
Instagram and Twitter: @youthservice
YSA helps increase the number and quality of
volunteer opportunities for young people at
thousands of organizations.

Dillon, Molly. *Yes She Can: 10 Stories of Hope & Change from Young Female Staffers of the Obama White House.* New York, NY: Schwartz & Wade, 2019.

Falkowski, Melissa, and Eric Garner, eds. *We Say #NeverAgain: Reporting by the Parkland Student Journalists.* New York, NY: Crown Books for Young Readers, 2018.

Feltus, William J., and Dallek Goldstein. *Inside Campaigns: Elections through the Eyes of Political Professionals.* 2nd ed. Washington, DC: CQ Press, 2018.

Freedman, Lawrence. *Strategy: A History.* Reprint ed. New York, NY: Oxford University Press, 2015.

Goodwin, Doris Kearns. *Team of Rivals: The Political Genius of Abraham Lincoln.* New York, NY: Simon & Schuster, 2006.

Litman, Amanda, with foreword by Hillary Rodham Clinton. *Run for Something: A Real-Talk Guide to Fixing the System Yourself.* New York, NY: Atria Books, 2017.

Mutch, Robert E. *Campaign Finance: What Everyone Needs to Know.* New York, NY: Oxford University Press, 2016.

Obama, Barack. *The Audacity of Hope: Thoughts on Reclaiming the American Dream.* Reprint ed. New York, NY: Vintage, 2008.

Sun Tzu. *The Art of War.* Scotts Valley, CA: CreateSpace Independent Publishing Platform, 2018.

Tokaji, Daniel. *Election Law in a Nutshell* (Nutshells). St. Paul, MN: West Academic Publishing, 2017.

BIBLIOGRAPHY

Acevedo, Nicole. "Gen Z Activists Target Youth Ahead of Midterms with #WhyDoYouVote Campaign." NBC News, October 19, 2018. https://www.nbcnews .com/news/latino/gen-z-activists-target-youth-ahead -midterms-whydoyouvote-campaign-n920801.

American Association of Political Consultants. "40 under 40." Retrieved February 10, 2019. https:// theaapc.org/awards/40-under-40.

Bailey, Holly. "Steve Schmidt: The Man Behind McCain." *Newsweek*, October 10, 2018. https:// www.newsweek.com/steve-schmidt-man-behind -mccain-92215.

Beck, Julie, and Caroline Kitchener. "Early Signs of a Youth Wave." *The Atlantic*, November 6, 2018. https://www.theatlantic.com/politics/archive/2018/11 /youth-turnout-midterm-2018/575092.

Broockman, David E., and Evan J. Soltas. "A Natural Experiment on Discrimination in Elections." Stanford University Graduate School of Business Research Paper No. 3499. Revised October 10, 2018. https:// papers.ssrn.com/sol3/papers.cfm?abstract _id=2919664.

Cicero, Marcus Tullius. "Marcus Tullius Cicero, Letters of Marcus Tullius Cicero: with his Treatises on Friendship and Old Age, and Letters of Gaius Plinius Caecilius Secundus [1909]." Online Library of Liberty. Retrieved February 10, 2019. https://oll.libertyfund.org/titles/cicero-letters-of -marcus-tullius-cicero/simple.

CIRCLE: The Center for Information and Research on Civic Learning and Engagement. "An Estimated 24 Million Young People Voted in 2016 Election."

Retrieved February 5, 2019. https://civicyouth.org
/an-estimated-24-million-young-people-vote-in-2016
-election.

CIRCLE: The Center for Information and Research on
Civic Learning and Engagement. "New Census Data
Confirm Increase in Youth Voter Turnout in 2008."
April 28, 2009. https://civicyouth.org/new-census
-data-confirm-increase-in-youth-voter-turnout-in
-2008-election.

CSPAN. "Presidential Historians Survey." Retrieved
February 4, 2019. https://www.c-span.org
/presidentsurvey2017.

Dingfelder, Sadie. "The Science of Political
Advertising." American Psychological Association,
Monitor on Psychology 43, no. 4 (April 2012): 46.
https://www.apa.org/monitor/2012/04/advertising.

Elliff, John T. "Views of the Wigwam Convention: Letters
from the Son of Lincoln's 1856 Candidate." *Journal
of the Abraham Lincoln Association* 33, no. 2
(Summer 2010): 1–11. http://hdl.handle.net/2027
/spo.2629860.0031.203.

FairVote. "Lower the Voting Age for Local Elections."
Retrieved February 12, 2019. https://www.fairvote
.org/lower_the_voting_age.

File, Tom. "Voting in America: A Look at the 2016
Presidential Election." United States Census Bureau,
Social, Economic, and Housing Statistics Division,
May 10, 2017. https://www.census.gov/newsroom
/blogs/random-samplings/2017/05/voting_in
_america.html.

Fredericks, Bob. "Clinton's Campaign Staff Is Five
Times the Size of Trump's." *New York Post*, October
7, 2016. https://nypost.com/2016/10/07/clintons
-campaign-staff-is-five-times-the-size-of-trumps.

Galanes, Philip. "Hillary Clinton and America Ferrera on Pain and Progress (and Hiking)." *New York Times*, September 16, 2017. https://www.nytimes .com/2017/09/16/style/hillary-clinton-america-ferrera -table-for-three.html.

Gallup. "Understanding Gallup's Likely Voter Procedures for Presidential Elections." Retrieved February 15, 2019. https://news.gallup.com/poll/111268/How -Gallups-likely-voter-models-work.aspx.

History, Art & Archives: United States House of Representatives. "Whereas: Stories from the People's House." November 21, 2016. https://history .house.gov/Blog/2016/November/11-21-Candidate -Congresswoman.

Jackson, David J. "The Effects of Celebrity Endorsements of Ideas and Presidential Candidates." *Journal of Political Marketing,* September 28, 2018. https://www.tandfonline.com /doi/full/10.1080/15377857.2018.1501530.

Jordan, Mary, and Scott Clement. "Rallying Nation: In Reaction to Trump, Millions of Americans Are Joining Protests and Getting Political." *Washington Post*, April 6, 2018. https://www.washingtonpost.com /news/national/wp/2018/04/06/feature/in-reaction-to -trump-millions-of-americans-are-joining-protests-and -getting-political.

Kaczynski, Andrew, and Nathan McDermott. "Rep. Mia Love's Campaign Admits to Improperly Raising Primary Election Funds." CNN, September 10, 2018. https://www.cnn.com/2018/09/10/politics/mia-love -campaign-funds/index.html.

Kaplan, Jonas T., Sarah Gimbel, and Sam Harris. "Neural Correlates of Maintaining One's Political

Beliefs in the Face of Counterevidence." *Scientific Reports*, no 6 (December 23, 2016), article number 39589.https://www.nature.com/articles/srep39589.

Karson, Kendall. "They Can't Vote, but These Kansas Teens Are Running for Governor." ABC News, August 7, 2018. https://abcnews.go.com/Politics/vote-kansas-teens-running-governor/story?id=57058542.

Maxwell, Angie, and Todd Shields. "The Impact of 'Modern Sexism' on the 2016 Presidential Election." Retrieved February 7, 2019. https://blaircenter.uark.edu/the-impact-of-modern-sexism.

Pew Research Center. "A Deep Dive into Party Affiliation." April 7, 2015. http://www.people-press.org/2015/04/07/a-deep-dive-into-party-affiliation.

Population Reference Bureau (PRB). "Who Votes in America?" October 1, 2006. https://www.prb.org/whovotesinamerica.

Rosentiel, Tom. "Young Voters in the 2008 Election." Pew Research Center, November 13, 2008. http://www.pewresearch.org/2008/11/13/young-voters-in-the-2008-election.

Smith, Rosa Inocencio. "Taylor Swift's Post-*Reputation* Approach to Politics." *The Atlantic,* October 10, 2018. https://www.theatlantic.com/entertainment/archive/2018/10/taylor-swift-gets-political/572683.

Sun Tzu. *The Art of War.* Scotts Valley, CA: CreateSpace Independent Publishing Platform, 2018.

Venugopal, Arun. "Why Alexandria Ocasio-Cortez Won." WNYC, June 27, 2018. https://www.wnyc.org/story/why-alexandria-ocasio-cortez-won.

INDEX

ABOUT THE AUTHOR

Melissa Banigan is the founder and CEO of Advice Project Media, a nonprofit that offers journalism training for teens, youth, and women around the world. An author and educator, she has taught and lectured about gender equality, feminism, and teen rights in the United States, Cameroon, Peru, and Guadeloupe. Also a multimedia journalist, Banigan has bylines in many national and international publications, including the *Washington Post*, CNN, NPR, and the BBC. Her first book, *Coping with Teen Pregnancy* (Rosen Publishing), was released in January 2019.

PHOTO CREDITS

Cover Steve Debenport/E+/Getty Images; pp. 4–5 (background graphics) weerawan/iStock/Getty Images; p. 5 Andrew Lichtenstein/Corbis News/Getty Images; p. 9 AFP/Getty Images; p. 10 DEA Picture Library/DeAgostini/Getty Images; p. 13 Library of Congress Rare Book And Special Collections Division; p. 15 Saul Loeb/AFP/Getty Images; p. 17 Don Emmert/AFP/Getty Images; p. 19 Joe Raedle/Getty Images; p. 22 stock_photo_world/Shutterstock.com; p. 25 Tom Williams/CQ Roll Call/Getty Images; p. 27 (inset) NY Daily News Archive/Getty Images; p. 29 Jupiterimages/PHOTOS.com/Getty Images; pp. 32, 37 Bloomberg/Getty Images; p. 34 Mario Tama/Getty Images; pp. 39, 51 The Boston Globe/Getty Images; p. 41 Bettmann/Getty Images; p. 43 Alex Wong/Getty Images; p. 46 Robyn Beck/AFP/Getty Images; p. 49 Thomas Trutschel/Photothek/Getty Images; additional graphic elements moodboard - Mike Watson Images/Brand X Pictures/Getty Images (chapter opener backgrounds), Maksim M/Shutterstock.com (fists).

Design and Layout: Michael Moy; Editor: Rachel Aimee; Photo Researcher: Nicole DiMella